A gift of
Friendship ...

To : Simona
From : Amber ♡

Christmas 2015

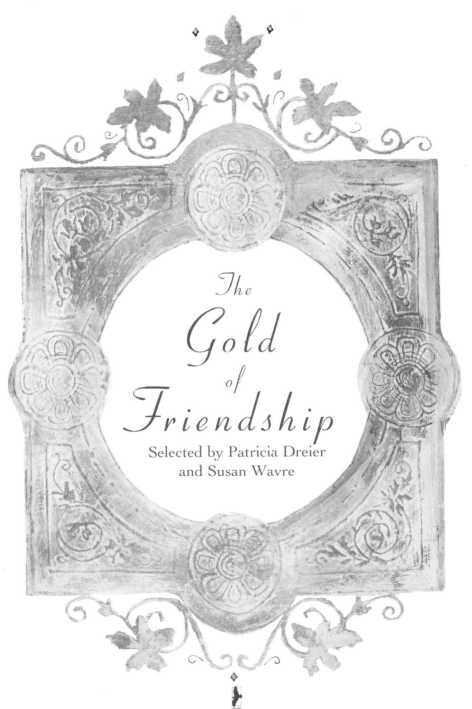

The
Gold
of
Friendship

Selected by Patricia Dreier
and Susan Wavre

Eagle Publishing, Guildford, Surrey, UK

Tulipa aurei coloris
Tulipa aurei coloris
Tulipa
Tulipa aurei coloris
Tulipa

Tulipa aurei coloris

IV.

True Friend

When you don't feel that you have
  to be perfect to be accepted,
When you are given the freedom
  to be yourself in every situation,
When you ask for an opinion
  knowing that you'll be told the truth,
When you share your heart
  without the risk of betrayal,
When being together is
  more important than what you do . . .
That is when you're
  in the presence of a true friend.
                        Roy Lessin

You can always tell a real friend:
when you've made a fool of yourself he doesn't
feel you've done a permanent job.
                        Laurence J. Peter

That Good and Timely Deed

Friendships do not come by chance. Upon the looms of circumstances Fate weaves an intricate design – and threads of other lives entwine to make a pattern with our own. We were not made to walk alone. Our pathways lead to where we meet a friend in need. It seems that it was meant to be. And how important is that little touch of kindness at a time when it is needed most. These are kindnesses that you don't forget: the gesture of true sympathy that's made in all sincerity and comes when you are weary or upset. The understanding word that reaches down into your heart – at the very moment of your need. A well-timed act of friendliness that saves you from despair – even though it may be small. A good turn done for you that shows that someone has concern for you. How much it really means – that good and timely deed! The love that we appreciate is that which does not come too late to help us when we need it most of all!

Author unknown

Friendship

Friendship becomes a great adventure. There is a continuously deeper discovery of myself and my friend, as we continue to reveal new and deeper layers of ourselves. It opens my mind, widens my horizons, fills me with new awareness, deepens my feelings, gives my life meaning.

John Powell

Love forgets mistakes; nagging about them parts the best of friends.

Proverbs 17:9

A faithful friend is the medicine of life.

Ecclesiasticus 6:16

Faithful Friend

Some paint lovely pictures,
   Others write good books,
Some make peaceful gardens,
   Others are fine cooks.
But the talent that endureth,
   That matters in the end,
Is the tenderness and caring
   That makes a faithful friend.
                    Jean Harris

Love Is Like the Wild Rose-Briar

Love is like the wild rose-briar;
Friendship like the holly-tree.
The holly is dark when the rose-briar blooms,
But which will bloom most constantly.
                    Emily Brontë

The Heart of a Friend

If, instead of a gem or even a flower, we could
cast the gift of a lovely thought into the heart of a
friend, that would be giving as angels give.

George MacDonald

When the Heart Runs Over

We cannot tell the precise moment when friendship is formed. As in filling a vessel drop by
drop, there is at last a drop which makes the
heart run over.

James Boswell

Enjoy Each Other

Oh, God, we go through life so lonely, needing
what other people can give us, yet ashamed to
show that need.

And other people go through life so lonely,
hungering for what it would be such a joy for
us to give.

Dear God, please bring us together, the
people who need each other, who can help each
other, and would so enjoy each other.

Marjorie Holmes

Of all the things which provides to make life
entirely happy, much the greatest is the
possession of friendship.

Epicurus

Make no mistake about it,
responsibilities toward other
human beings are the greatest
blessings God can send us.
                Dorothy Dix

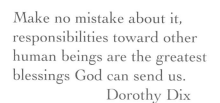

✿✿✿✿✿✿

If a man does not make new acquaintance as he
advances through life, he will soon find himself left
alone. A man, Sir, should keep his friendship in
constant repair.
                        Dr Samuel Johnson

✿✿✿✿✿✿

If we would build on a sure foundation in friendship, we must love friends for their sake rather
than for our own.
                        Charlotte Brontë

Golden Ties of Friendship

A friend is like a tower strong;
a friend is like the joyous song
    that helps us on our way.
      When golden ties
      of friendship bind
      the heart to heart,
      the mind to mind,
        how fortunate are we!

For friendship is a noble thing;
it soars past death on angel's wing
    into eternity.
God blesses friendship's holy bond
both here and in the great beyond:
    a benefit unpriced.
      Then may we know
      that wondrous joy,
that precious ore without alloy;
    a friendship based on Christ.

                Kevin Mayhew

HYDRANGEAS

Collected In The Late Summer Of 1876

Old Friendship

Beautiful and rich is an old friendship,
Grateful to the touch as ancient ivory,
Smooth as aged wine, or sheen
    of tapestry
Where light has lingered,
    intimate and long.
Full of tears and warm is an old
    friendship
That asks no longer deeds of
    gallantry,
Or any deed at all –
    save that the friend shall be
Alive and breathing somewhere,
    like a song.
Eunice Tietjens

❊ ❊ ❊ ❊ ❊ ❊ ❊ ❊

True friendship is the least jealous of loves.
C. S. Lewis

Thank You for My Friend

I don't believe I've ever thought to thank you,
God, for this wonderful friend. But I do thank
you for creating her and letting her enrich my life
this way.

Thank you for all the years we've known each
other and the confidences and hopes and troubles
that we've shared.

Thank you for the understanding we bring to
each other. For the patience we have with each
other's faults; for the advice and even the
scoldings we are able to give each other without
either of us taking offence.

Thank you for the help we have been to each
other – in this way, and so many more. Thank
you that because of her I am a better, happier
person, and that she has grown as a person
because of me.

Thank you that she would give me anything in
her power – time, money, work, possessions,
encouragement, sympathy – whatever my need.
And that she knows I would be as quick to
respond to whatever her needs might be.

Thank you that we can laugh together, cry together, rejoice together. And although we may not see each other for a long time, when we do come together it is always the same.

Lord, bless and keep her, this person you fashioned and filled with qualities that have meant so much to me. Lord, thank you for my friend.

Marjorie Holmes

✿ ✿ ✿ ✿ ✿ ✿

Friendship consists of forgetting what one gives, and remembering what one receives.
Alexandre Dumas

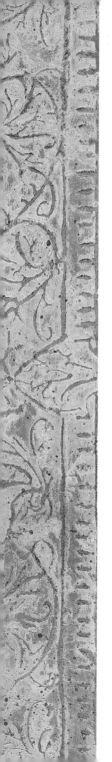

What Is Life Without a Friend?

Say not that friendship's but a name,
Sincere we none can find;
An empty bubble in the air,
A phantom of the mind.
What is life without a friend?
A dreary race to run,
A desert where no water is,
A world without a sun.
           Henry Alford

❀ ❀ ❀ ❀ ❀ ❀

'Stay' is the most charming word in
a friend's vocabulary.
           Amos Bronson Alcott

❀ ❀ ❀ ❀ ❀

A friend is someone who knows all about you and
likes you anyway.
           Christi Mary Warner

Types of Friendship

There are three friendships which are advantageous, and three which are injurious . . .
Friendship with the upright, with the sincere,
and with the man of much observation, these are
advantageous. Friendship with the man of
specious airs, with the insinuatingly soft, and with
the glib-tongued, these are injurious.

Confucius

At eighteen, friendship is the buoyant acceptance
of those who play and work and laugh and dream
together. As a man gets older, he wants friends to
stimulate him, to keep his mind active and young.

Bernard Baruch

Reserve robs us of our future friendships. Putting
up walls to protect ourselves robs us of love and
intimacy.

David Riddell

COLLECTED TREASURES

PAPILIO ULYSSES

She Is My Friend

She listens when I talk, but more than that, she always hears me. She hears the subtle shading in my voice that tells her what my words do not. She catches feelings, carefully concealed behind the words, and understands.

She is my friend, and so she doesn't damage my hurt pride by pointing out my frailities. She simply says a thoughtful word or two, and suddenly I'm able to accept, to speak aloud my worries and embarrassments. I talk to her, and as I do, my confidence returns.

Her friendship once again has shored me up, and I can face my fears and laugh them down. How many times she's listened when I talk, and how I count on her to really hear me.

Raphael Marie Turnbull

❊ ❊ ❊ ❊ ❊

Shared joy is double joy, and shared sorrow is half-sorrow.

Swedish proverb

Friend

A warm handclasp,
  A fond embrace,
  A friendly smile
When face to face –
A cheerful greeting
Which seems to say
That you're concerned
  This makes my day.

I sense a gladness
  When we meet
  Upon the stair
Or on the street.
Your sparkling eye –
  This simple act
Makes glad my heart,
  Now, that's a fact.

Louis Everett Downing

Count Your Friends

Count your garden by the flowers,
Never by the leaves that fall;
Count your days by golden hours,
Don't remember clouds at all.
Count your nights by stars, not shadows,
Count your years with smiles, not tears,
Count your blessings, not your
    troubles,
Count your age by friends, not
    years.

Author unknown

Friendship with Oneself

Friendship with oneself is all
important, because without it one
cannot be friends with anyone else in
the world.

Eleanor Roosevelt

A Friend Is . . .

A friend is someone who helps you clean up the dishes and you don't even have to protest once.

. . . that one word 'hello' over the phone that can make you feel better than 10 minutes of conversation with anyone else.

. . . deep talk that goes on until 3 a.m. On a work night!

A friend is more than a shoulder to cry on. A friend is the kind of understanding that makes crying unnecessary.

. . . someone to call in a hurry when something really watchable is on TV.

. . . sharing a pizza.

A friend is someone you can do nothing with and enjoy it.

. . . one good reason for believing in ESP.

. . . someone who won't say, 'You look terrible!' when you look terrible.

A friend is the one who is already there doing it when everyone else is saying, 'Is there anything I can do?'

. . . someone who will quietly destroy the snapshot that makes you look like the bride of Frankenstein.

. . . not too much sugar and just enough spice.

A friend is the kind of person who never wants to dress alike.

. . . someone who dislikes the same people you do.

. . . a little bit different every day but always the same.

A friend is someone who really is glad when you succeed.

. . . a believer in the spur of the moment.

. . . someone with whom you can either a borrower or a lender be.

A friend is a person who knows your sensitive spots but will never poke you there.

. . . a whole lot of wonderful people rolled into one.

. . . someone you can trade secrets with and never worry.

. . . laughter and going places and doing new things and having the best time ever.

A friend is the closest thing to me there is in more ways than one.

Gayle Lawrence

CAMELLIA

The first camellias were imported into Europe in the mid eighteenth century. They were brought over from China, Japan, Korea and Burma where they were growing wild.

The camellia flowers from late winter to spring

fig 16

JAPONICA

As of Old

The roads we chose diverged so little at the setting
    out and seemed so nearly side by side!
A little while we spoke across the way, then
     waved our
     hands,
     and then . . .
The hills between, life's other voices
    and the nights,
The silences . . .

Old friend, no new friend takes your place
With me as well
The hours and days flow by and lengthen into years,
But I do not forget. And not a thought that you have
    had of me –
Whether you wrote or spoke it, or, more like,
Just thought of me and let it go at that –
But it came winging through the silences!

Wherever you are, across the distance I give you my
    hand,
With my love as of old.

John Palmer Gavit

Friends Are Not a One-Way Street

Aren't friendships, on whatever level, a part of
human fortune? Friendships can be infinitely
varied, and by their very differentness the whole
pattern of one's days can be enlivened, and in so
many ways rewarding.

Sift through your friendships; sort them.

There is the rich inner circle of those people
who are dearest to the heart. Usually these are
the persons to whom we can most honestly
express our deepest selves. And even though we
may not see them for days, weeks on end – even
years – the bond remains strong and special and
true.

Yet would we not be the poorer without the
infinite variety of others?

Friends can be friends for so many different
reasons.

There is the wonderfully helpful neighbour
who is always willing to give you a
hand with the children.

There is the witty one who can
always make you laugh.

There is the one who sends over bones for the dog, and is generous with praise for your growing crew.

There is the quiet soul who occasionally comes up with a startling gem of philosophy.

It takes patience sometimes to appreciate the true values in the people with whom circumstances have surrounded us. It takes awareness to recognize these values when they appear.

Yet almost everyone has something uniquely his own to contribute to our lives – and equally important, a place in his own life that perhaps we alone can satisfy.

The heart has many doors. Don't be too quick to bolt them.

Marjorie Holmes

Unselfish Friendship

Friendship needs no studied phrases,
Polished face, or winning wiles;
Friendship deals no lavish praises,
Friendship dons no surface smiles.
Friendship follows Nature's diction,
Shuns the blandishments of Art,
Boldly severs truth from fiction,
Speaks the language of the heart.
Friendship – pure, unselfish friendship,
All through life's allotted span,
Nurtures, strengthens, widens, lengthens,
Man's relationship with man.

Author unknown

No person is your friend who demands your
silence, or denies your right to grow.

Alice Walker

Everyone Needs Friends

Without friends no one would choose to live, though he had all other goods; even rich men and those in possession of office and of dominating power are thought to need friends most of all; for what is the use of such prosperity without the opportunity of beneficence, which is exercised chiefly and in its most laudable form toward friends?

Or how can prosperity be guarded and preserved without friends? The greater it is, the more exposed is it to risk. And in poverty and in other misfortunes men think friends are the only refuge. It helps the young, too, to keep from error; it aids older people by ministering to their needs and supplementing the activities that are failing from weakness; those in the prime of life it stimulates to noble actions . . . for with friends men are more able both to think and to act.

Aristotle

What do we live for, if it is not to make life less difficult for each other?

George Eliot

Spring time tulips

GLORIA IN EXCELSIS DEO

Gloria in excelsis deo

A Friend Listens

I have noted that the best and closest friends are those who seldom call on each other for help. In fact, such is almost the finest definition of a friend – a person who does not need us but who is able to enjoy us.

I have seldom suffered over the troubles of a friend. Are his mishaps short of tragedy, I am inclined to chuckle. And he is seldom serious in telling me of his misfortunes. He makes anecdotes out of them, postures comically in their midst and tries to entertain me with them. This is one of the chief values of my friendship, as it is of his. We enable each other to play the strong man superior to his fate.

Given a friend to listen, my own disasters change colour. I win victories while relating them. Not only have I a friend on my side who will believe my version of the battle – and permit me to seem a victor in my communiques – but I have actually a victory in me. I am able to show my friend my untouched side. My secret superiority to bad events becomes stronger when I can speak and have a friend believe in it.

Ben Hecht

The Things I Prize

These are the things I prize
And hold of dearest worth:
Light of the sapphire skies,
Peace of the silent hills,
Shelter of the forests, comfort of the grass,
Music of birds, murmur of little rills,
Shadows of clouds that swiftly pass,
And, after showers,
The smell of flowers
And of the good brown earth –
And best of all, along the way, friendship and
     mirth.

Henry Van Dyke

✿ ✿ ✿ ✿ ✿

It takes two to make a quarrel, but
only one to end it.

Spanish proverb

Changing Lives

People's lives change. To keep all your old
friends is like keeping all your old clothes -
pretty soon your closet is so jammed and everything so crushed you can't find anything to
wear. Help these friends when they need you;
bless the years and happy times when you
meant a lot to each other, but try not to have
the guilts if new people mean more to you now.

Helen Gurley Brown

Don't Try to Live Alone

The person who tries to live alone will not succeed as a human being. His heart withers if it
does not answer another heart. His mind
shrinks away if he hears only the echoes of his
own thoughts and finds no other inspiration.

Pearl Buck

Giving

There isn't much that I can do,
But I can sit an hour with you,
And I can share a joke with you,
And sometimes reverses, too . . .
    As on our way we go.
            Maude V. Preston

For happiness brings happiness,
and loving ways bring love,
And giving is the treasure
that contentment is made of.
        Amanda Bradley

❀ ❀ ❀ ❀ ❀ ❀

There is an important difference between love
and friendship. While the former delights in
extremes and opposites, the latter demands
equality.
        Françoise d'Aubigne Maintenon

Sharing

There isn't much that I can do,
But I can share my flowers with you,
And I can share my books with you,
And sometimes share your burdens, too . . .
  As on our way we go.
          Maude V. Preston

Sharing the Good and the Bad

We may describe friendly feeling towards anyone as wishing for him what you believe to be good things, not for your own sake but for his, and being inclined, so far as you can, to bring these things about. A friend is one who feels thus and excites these feelings in return: those who think they feel thus towards each other think themselves friends.

This being assumed, it follows that your friend is the sort of man who shares your pleasure in what is good and your pain in what is unpleasant, for your sake and for no other reason. This pleasure and pain of his will be the token of his good wishes for you, since we all feel glad at getting what we wish for, and pained at getting what we do not. Those, then, are friends to whom the same things are good and evil.

          Aristotle

Begin the Day with Friendliness

Begin the day with friendliness and only friends
you'll find . . .

    Yes, greet the dawn with happiness, keep happy
thoughts in mind . . . Salute the day with peaceful
thoughts and peace will fill your heart . . .

    Begin the day with joyful soul and joy will be
your part . . .

    Begin the day with friendliness, keep friendly
all day long . . . Keep in your soul a friendly
thought, your heart a friendly song . . . Have in
your mind a world of cheer for all who come your
way . . . And they will bless you too, in turn, and
wish you 'Happy Day!' . . .

    Begin each day with friendly thoughts and as
the day goes on . . . Keep friendly, loving, good and
kind just as you were at dawn . . . The day will be a
friendly one and then at night you'll find . . . That
you were happy all day through friendly thoughts
in mind.

                             Author unknown

A Time to Be Silent

There may be moments in friendship, as in love,
when silence is beyond words. The faults of our
friend may be clear to us, but it is well to seem
to shut our eyes to them. Friendship is usually
treated by the majority of mankind as a tough
and everlasting thing which will survive all
manner of bad treatment. But this is an exceed-
ingly great and foolish error; it may die in an
hour of a single unwise word; its conditions of
existence are that it should be dealt with deli-
cately and tenderly, being as it is a sensible
plant and not a roadside thistle. We must not
expect our friend to be above humanity.

Ouida

Choice of Friends

True happiness
Consists not in the multitude of friends,
But in the worth and choice.

Ben Jonson

Love a Friend for Himself

The love of friendship should be gratuitous.
You ought not to have or to love a friend for
what he will give you. If you love him for the
reason that he will supply you
with money or some other
temporal favour, you love the
gift rather than him. A friend
should be loved freely for himself, and not for anything else.

St Augustine

Golden Thread of Friendship

There is in friendship something of all relations, and something above them all. It is the
golden thread that tied the hearts of all
hearts of all the world.

John Evelyn

The Blessing of Friendship

A blessed thing it is for any man or woman to
have a friend; one human soul whom we can
trust utterly; who knows the best and the worst
of us, and who loves us in spite of all our
faults; who will speak the honest truth to us,
while the world flatters us to our face, and
laughs at us behind our back; who will give us
counsel and reproof in the day of prosperity
and self-conceit; but who, again, will comfort
and encourage us in the day of difficulty and
sorrow, when the world leaves us alone to fight
our own battle as we can.

Charles Kingsley

Because of a Friend

Because of a friend, life is a little stronger,
fuller, more gracious thing for the friend's
existence, whether he be near or far. If the
friend is close at hand, that is best; but if he is
far away he still is there to think of, to wonder
about, to hear from, to write to, to share life
and experience with, to serve, to honour, to
admire, to love.

Arthur Christopher Benson

At All Hours

The most agreeable of all companions is a simple
frank person, without any high pretensions to an
oppressive greatness – one who loves life, and
understands the use of it; obliging alike at all
hours; above all, of a golden temper, and stead-
fast as an anchor. For such a one we gladly
exchange the greatest genius, the most brilliant
wit, the profoundest thinker.
                    Gotthold Ephraim Lessing

It is the friends you can call at 4 a.m. that matter.
        Marlene Dietrich

The Hours that Truly Count

Life may scatter us and keep us apart; it may prevent us from thinking very often of one another; but we know that our comrades are somewhere 'out there' – where, one can hardly say – silent, forgotten, but deeply faithful. And when our paths cross theirs, they greet us with such manifest joy, shake us so gaily by the shoulders!

Indeed we are accustomed to waiting . . .
We forget that there is no hope of joy except in human relations. If I summon up those memories that have left me with an enduring savour, if I draw up the balance sheet of the hours in my life that have truly counted, surely I find only those that no wealth could have procured me.

True richness cannot be bought.

Antoine de Saint-Exupery

A friend loves at all times.

Proverbs 17:17

An Understanding Heart

On the level of the human spirit an equal, a companion, an understanding heart is one who can share a man's point of view. What this means we all know. Friends, companions, lovers, are those who treat us in terms of our unlimited worth to ourselves. They are closest to us who best understand what life means to us, who feel for us as we feel for ourselves, who are bound to us in triumph and disaster, who break the spell of our loneliness.

Henry Alonzo Myers

Reprove a friend in secret, but praise him before others.
Leonardo da Vinci

Glory of Friendship

The glory of friendship is not the outstretched
hand, nor the kindly smile, nor the joy of com-
panionship; it is the spiritual inspiration that
comes to one when he discovers that someone
believes in him and is willing to trust him with
his friendship.

Ralph Waldo Emerson

Learn to Receive

It is more blessed to give than to receive . . .
(But) the givers who can not take in return
miss one of the finest graces in life, the grace
of receiving . . . To receive gratefully from
others is to enhance their sense of their worth.
it puts them on a give-and-take level, the only
level on which real fellowship can be
sustained. It changes one of the ugliest things
in the world, patronage, into one of the richest
things in the world, friendship.

Halford E. Luccock

Understanding and Trust

The very best thing is good talk, and the thing
that helps it most is friendship. How it dissolves
the barriers that divide us, and loosens all
constraints, and diffuses itself like some fine old
cordial through all the veins of life – this feeling
that we understand and trust each other, and
wish each other heartily well! Everything into
which it really comes is good. It transforms
letter writing from a task to a pleasure. It makes
music a thousand times more sweet. The people
who play and sing not at us, but to us – how
delightful it is to listen to them! Yes, there is a
talkability that can express itself even without
words. There is an exchange of thoughts and
feelings which is happily alike in speech and in
silence. It is quietness pervaded with friendship.

Henry van Dyke

❀ ❀ ❀ ❀ ❀ ❀

Give truth, and your gift will be paid in kind,
And honor will honor meet;
And the smile which is sweet will surely find
A smile that is just as sweet.

Madeline S. Bridges

Surrender to Time

It may seem, looking back, that becoming a friend . . . takes place in an instant. If we examine the experience, however, we discover that a long preparation through time precedes those moments which friends finally recognize and respond to each other. If we do not surrender to time, we may never recognize our true selves nor the true selves of others; we may not be able to enter those instants in which we see someone else in a way that no one else has ever seen them before . . .

Friends move toward each other through time. When they meet they are able to respond to all that they have come to recognize as valuable. Time is the tide that brings us together when we are ready for the challenge of friendship.

Eugene Kennedy

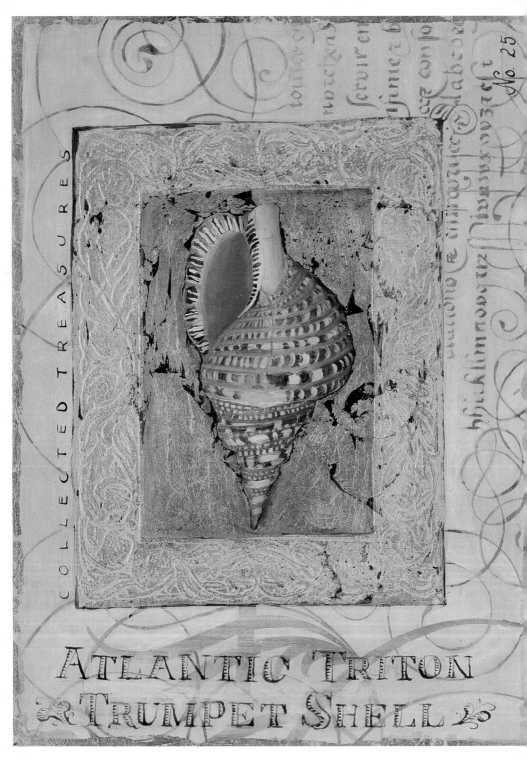

COLLECTED TREASURES

No. 25

ATLANTIC TRITON
TRUMPET SHELL

Special People

There are red-letter days in our lives when we meet
people who thrill us like a fine poem, people whose
handshake is brimful of unspoken sympathy and
whose sweet, rich natures impart to our eager,
impatient spirits a wonderful restfulness which is in its
essence divine . . .
Perhaps we never saw them before and they may
never cross our life's path again; but the influence of
their calm, mellow natures is a libation poured upon
our discontent, and we feel its healing touch as the
ocean feels the mountain stream freshening its brine . . .

Helen Keller

A Friend

Crossing the uplands of time,
Skirting the borders of night,
Scaling the face of the peak of dreams,
We enter the region of light,
And hastening on with eager intent,
Arrive at the rainbow's end,
And here uncover the pot of gold
Buried deep in the heart of a friend.

Grace Goodhue Coolidge

Friendship

There are marvellous joys in friendship. This is
easily understood as soon as one realizes that
joy is contagious. If my presence gives a friend
some real happiness, the sight of his happiness is
enough to make me in turn feel happy; thus the
joy that each of us gives is returned to him; at
the same time, vast reserves of joy are released;
both friends say to themselves: 'I had happiness
in me that I wasn't making use of.'

The source of happiness is within us, I'll
admit that; and there is nothing sadder to see
than people dissatisfied with themselves and
with everything else, and who have to tickle
each other in order to be able to laugh.
However, it must be added that a happy man
quickly forgets that he is happy once he is alone;
all his joy soon becomes numbed; he sinks into a
kind of unawareness bordering on stupor. An
inner feeling needs an external form of manifes-
tation. If some tyrant or other imprisoned me in
order to teach me respect for the mighty, I
would make it a rule of good health to laugh
every day all alone; I would exercise my joy just
as I would exercise my legs . . .

When a baby laughs for the first time, his laughter expresses nothing at all; he is not laughing because he is happy; instead I should say that he is happy because he is laughing; he enjoys laughing, just as he enjoys eating, but first he has to try eating. This is not only true for laughter; one needs words in order to know what one is thinking. As long as one is alone, one cannot be oneself. Simple-minded moralists say that loving means forgetting yourself; that is too simplistic; the more you get away from yourself, the more you are yourself; and the more you feel alive.

Alain

Acknowledgements

Alain, Alain on Happiness (Frederick Ungar Publishing Co.Inc.,1973).
cummings, e.e., in John Powell's, Why am I afraid to tell you I love you? (Allen, Texas: Argus Communications, 1969).
de Saint-Exupery, Antoine, Wind, Sand and Stars (Harcourt Brace Jovanovich, Inc., 1939).
Harris, Jean , quoted in Francis Gay's Friendship Book.
Hecht, Ben, A Child of the Century (Simon & Schuster, 1954).
Holmes, Marjorie, I've Got to Talk to Somebody, God (London: Hodder & Stoughton, 1969); and for 'Friends Are Not a One-Way Street' from Love and Laughter (Marjorie Holmes and Toni Mendez Inc. 1959, 1967).
Kennedy, Eugene, A Time for Being Human (Norwalk, CT.: C.R. Gibson, 1977).
Lessin, Roy, on a prayer card (Kingsway Communications Ltd.).
Lewis, C.S., The Four Loves (London: Fontana, 1963).
Luccock, Halford, Living Without Gloves, More Letters of Simeon Stylites (Oxford University Press, 1957).
Mayhew, Kevin, on a prayer card © Kevin Mayhew.
Myers, Henry Alonzo, Are Men Equal? (Cornell University Press, 1945).
Powell, John, Why am I afraid to tell you I love you? (Allen, Texas: Argus Communications, 1969).
Repplier, Agnes, seen in Marion Stroud, Gift of Friends (Oxford: Lion Publishing, 1983).]
Riddell, David, Living Wisdom (Guildford: Eagle Publishing, 1996).
Turnbull, Raphael Marie, Woman to Woman (Norwalk, CT.: C.R. Gibson, 1979).